TIDEWATER VIRGINIA

a photographic portrait

PHOTOGRAPHY BY

Jake McGuire

First published in the United States of
America by:

Twin Lights Publishers, Inc.
8 Hale Street
Rockport, Massachusetts 01966
Telephone: (978) 546-7398
http://www.twinlightspub.com

ISBN: 1-885435-72-X
ISBN: 978-1-885435-72-9

10 9 8 7 6 5 4 3 2 1

Hampton Harbor (opposite)

The Hampton River waterfront offers sites
of historic interest, residential high-rises
and marinas.

(jacket front)

Federal-style architecture in the Freemason
district

(jacket back)

The Schooner *Alliance*

Special thanks to Anna Katalkina for help-
ing to produce this book. She worked tire-
lessly on researching Tidewater subjects,
arranging and coordinating the shooting, as
well as selecting and photo editing many
hundreds of pictures. Anna is an accom-
plished artist, with works in private and
corporate collections in the U.S. and abroad.
Her fine art photography of Europe is a part
of The McGuire Collection.

Editorial researched and written by:
Francesca and Duncan Yates
www.freelancewriters.com

Book design by:
SYP Design & Production, Inc.
www.sypdesign.com

Printed in China

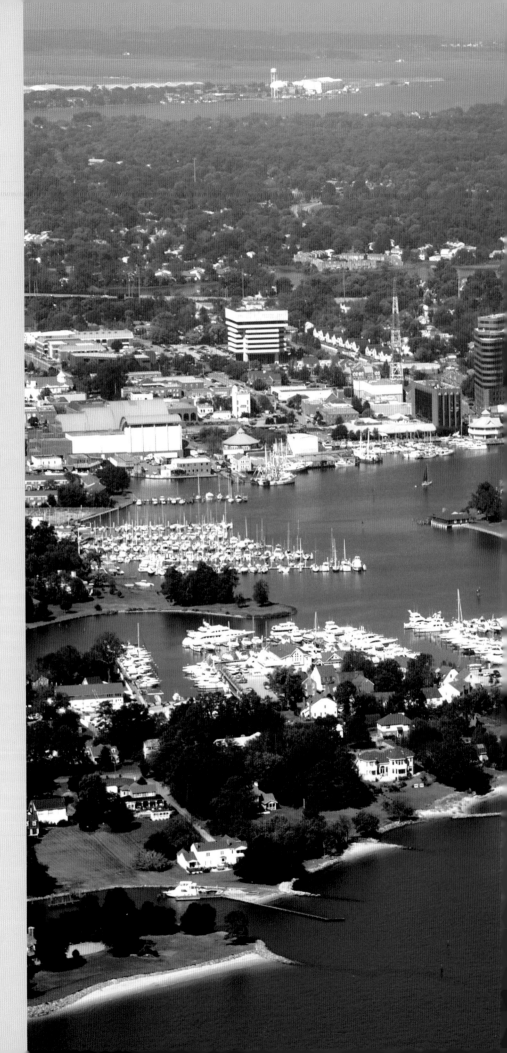

O n the shores of the Virginia Peninsula, American history began in 1607, when 101 English men and 4 boys, exhausted from their ocean crossing in three small ships, stepped ashore at Jamestown. More than a dozen previous efforts to colonize America had failed, yet Jamestown persevered to become the oldest permanent English settlement in the New World.

The Hampton, James, Elizabeth, and Nansemond Rivers meet in the body of water known as *Hampton Roads* before they empty into the Chesapeake. Taken from the English term for *harbor*, Hampton *Roads* is one of the greatest natural harbors in the world. It was only fitting that the companies in England that financed the venture chose this location for settlement. Soon after, the region would become the center of a thriving tobacco export industry. Today, the Tidewater area includes the seven cities of Hampton, Newport News, Norfolk, Chesapeake, Portsmouth, Suffolk, and Virginia Beach, as well as the historic communities of Yorktown, Jamestown, and Williamsburg.

Through the centuries, the tidewaters of Virginia have had a front-row seat for major historic battles and events that helped to shape the country. The last battle of the American Revolution was fought and won at Yorktown. The great sea battle of the ironclads during the Civil War was fought in Hampton Roads waters.

By land and by sea, the compelling images of award-winning photographer, Jake McGuire, introduce the historic cities and communities of Tidewater Virginia in this striking photographic portrait. Visit the triangle of historic colonial villages: Jamestown, Yorktown, and Colonial Williamsburg. Tour the quaint town of Hampton, the modern cities of Norfolk, home to the world's largest naval base; Newport News, the center of the military shipbuilding industry, and the resort city of Virginia Beach, the largest city in the state. Each location is rich in historic and cultural treasures, acclaimed universities and exciting entertainment venues.

From the Colonial Era to present day, the Virginia Tidewater region has made invaluable contributions to the history and aspirations of a great nation.

Hunter House Victorian Museum

Open the door to this historic house in Norfolk and enter the Victorian era when life moved at a slower pace. Now a museum, the 1894 house was restored in 1988 and showcases original furnishings of the Hunter family.

Hampton Coliseum (top)

With its distinctive architecture, the Hampton Coliseum sits like a king's crown on seventy-five acres of landscaped parkland and provides a versatile venue for events from Cirque du Soleil to motorcycle racing on ice.

Convention Center (bottom)

The Hampton Roads Convention Center sports a nautical look with canvas sails that catch the breeze. Between meetings, conventioneers enjoy a variety of shops and other attractions along the scenic waterfront.

Old Point Comfort Light (opposite)

This historic lighthouse was built in 1803 on the northern entrance to Hampton Roads near Fort Monroe. The beacon's important roles during the War of 1812 and the Civil War earned it a listing on the National Register of Historic Places.

W 93

OLD POINT
COMFORT LIGHT

The lighthouse, built in 1802, is the oldest standing structure at Fort Monroe. It remains an active navigational aid, the property of the U.S. Coast Guard. During the War of 1812, the tower was used as a lookout by a British invasion force while they attacked Washington. The adjacent house was the lightkeepers' quarters until the light was automated in 1973 when the house became Army property.

DEPARTMENT OF CONSERVATION AND NATURE RESERVES, 1995

7

Historic Fort Monroe

Constructed in 1834, Fort Monroe was one of several coastal forts established to protect America from foreign invasion in the aftermath of the War of 1812 with Great Britain. Named for President James Monroe, the six-sided fort is completely surrounded by a moat and is the largest stone fort in the country. It remains an active U.S. Army post to this day. Walking tours of this historic site are offered during the summer months.

Casemate Museum

Fort Monroe's Casemate Museum is rich in Civil War artifacts and provides a fascinating showcase of how a young country learned to defend its shores. History buffs will appreciate the displays of uniforms, weapons, artillery and old photographs. The museum also features the quarters of a young lieutenant named Robert E. Lee, the guest quarters of President Abraham Lincoln and the prison cell of Confederate President Jefferson Davis.

Flags at Fort Monroe *(top)*

Fort Monroe has been a military post since the first English settlers arrived in 1609. Garrisoned continuously since 1823, this National Historic Landmark will officially close forever in 2011.

Engineers' Wharf *(bottom)*

A popular fishing pier today, Engineers' Wharf was built in 1818 to receive materials for the construction of Fort Monroe. The fort went on to play a significant role in the strategic advance of Union troops to pivotal victories during the Civil War.

Generals' Row *(opposite)*

Generals' Row is a prestigious, four-star neighborhood at Fort Monroe where the presiding generals of this historic army base have their living quarters. Today, the base's commanding officers oversee a broad military training operation.

Fort Wool *(above and left)*

Fort Wool, an important line of defense for the Tidewater area in early America, has been a state park since 1970. Early in the 20th century, Battery Ferdinand Claiborne, one of six batteries at Fort Wool, housed two shielded, six-inch disappearing guns pointing out to sea. Today scenic Fort Wool, along with its variety of coastal birds and native wildlife, is only accessible by boat and passenger ferry from Hampton.

Rocky Fortress

Originally named Fort Calhoun, this military post was built on rocky Rip-Raps Island in 1823. During the War of 1812 its coastal fortifications proved inadequate when the British were able to sail inland and burn Washington D.C. to the ground.

Hampton Waterfront *(top)*

Hampton's historic waterfront features cobblestone streets, a seaside park, and the famed Cousteau Society's world headquarters. The main exhibit area showcases the impressive contributions of famed undersea explorer Jacques-Yves Cousteau.

Hampton History Museum *(bottom)*

The Hampton History Museum and Visitor Center chronicles four hundred years of the oldest continuous English-speaking settlement in America. Nine galleries display artifacts from the Kecoughtan Indians through modern times.

American Theatre

Like many vaudeville houses, this 1908 theatre in the Phoebus area of Hampton, soon became a movie cinema. It was renovated in 2000 and is once again a top performing arts theatre with cutting edge acoustics and turn-of-the-century ambiance.

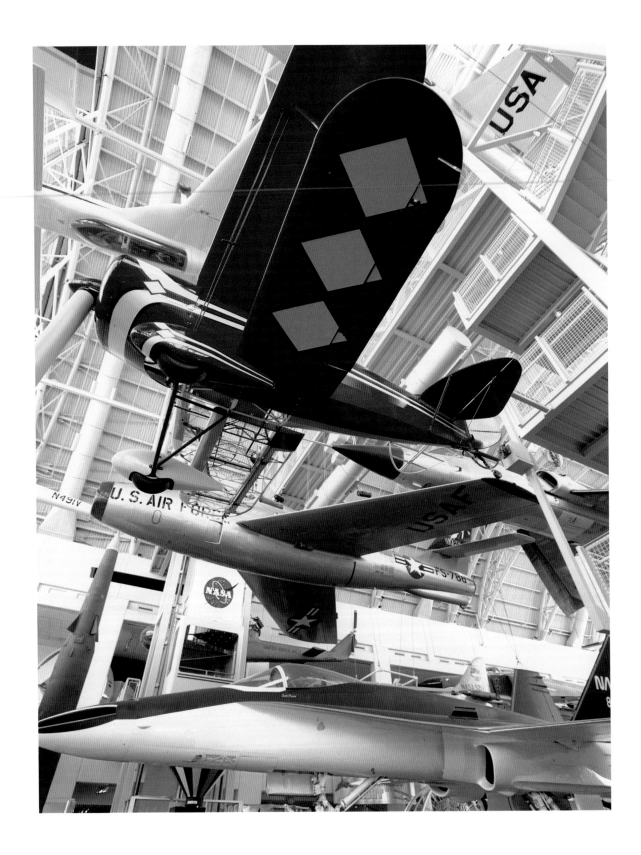

Adventures in Flight *(above)*

The 1903 Wright-Flyer, WW II Bombers and FA-22's are a sampling of the many aircraft on display at the Virginia Air and Space Center. Through simulation, one can experience the thrill of taking off from an aircraft carrier or piloting a space shuttle.

Virginia Air and Space Center *(opposite)*

The Virginia Air and Space Center celebrates Hampton Roads' important role in commercial, civil and military aeronautics. Interactive exhibits showcase historic moments in aviation from the Wright Brothers' inaugural flight to lunar orbits, rockets, the Apollo 12 Command Module and the Viking Lander that took the first photograph of the surface of Mars. The museum also features an IMAX theater. Nearby is the prestigious NASA Langley Research Center.

Marina Sunrise (*opposite*)

One of the friendliest communities on the Chesapeake Bay, Hampton is home to commercial fishermen as well as yachting enthusiasts attracted by weekly dockside concerts, harbor cruises, and a festival devoted to the infamous pirate, Blackbeard.

Osprey on Hampton River (*above*)

Impressive osprey are often found nesting along the Hampton River. With a wingspan of over five feet, the osprey is one of the largest birds of prey in North America. Diving in feet first to catch its quarry, the osprey dines almost exclusively on fish.

Sailing in Hampton Roads (opposite, top)

Winds from the bay fill sails during a glorious day of recreational boating in Hampton Roads.

Sport Fishing (opposite, bottom)

The Chesapeake Bay is a great venue for Atlantic sports fishermen, offering a variety of catches such as bass, rockfish and perch. The rich diversity of marine life also includes crabs, oysters, and eels. In the background is Naval Station Norfolk.

Farmers of the Sea (above)

Commercial fishing vessels deliver their catches to a seafood processing plant on the Hampton waterfront. The Hampton Roads fishing industry provides some of the freshest and sweetest Atlantic seafood on the coast.

Hampton University *(top)*

Hampton University was founded in 1868 after the Civil War to help former slaves learn the skills of self-sufficiency that came with their new freedom. Today the university has a student population of nearly six thousand.

Hampton University Museum *(bottom)*

Established in 1868, this landmark institution is the oldest African-American museum in the country, with permanent collections of over 9,000 artifacts and art that also represent cultures from Hawaii, the Pacific Islands, Asia and Africa.

Memorial Chapel Bell Tower *(opposite)*

Built in 1886 in the Italian Romanesque Revival style, the revered Memorial Chapel now serves as a non-denominational sanctuary on the Hampton University campus.

Volvo Ocean Race *(above and opposite)*

Some of the most skilled sailors in the world compete in this grueling, round-the-world race. The 2006 race course began in Galicia, Spain and ran to South Africa, Australia, South America, then on to Baltimore, New York, and across the Atlantic to Portsmouth, Rotterdam and Gothenburg. Spectators on Virginia Beach and the Hampton waterfront enjoyed exciting views of the race as these impressive vessels sailed with grace and speed through Chesapeake Bay to Baltimore.

James River's Gold Coast *(top)*

Luxury homes along the James River in Newport News are prime real estate with waterfront access, spectacular views of the river and bay, and the constant activities of naval, commercial, and recreational ships of all sizes.

Virginia Living Museum *(bottom)*

The Virigina Living Museum encompasses a native wildlife park, botanical preserve, science museum, planetarium, and aquarium. It became the first *living museum* east of the Mississippi in 1987 and continues to flourish with award-winning exhibits.

James River Bridge

When the James River Bridge was completed in 1928, it was the longest bridge over water in the world. Spanning 4.5 miles, it carries four lanes of traffic connecting the South Hampton Roads area to Newport News on the Virginia Peninsula.

Mariners' Museum *(above)*

This internationally acclaimed museum in Newport News is one of the largest and most comprehensive maritime museums in the world. Over 35,000 antiquities bear witness to the exciting history of the world's ships in both war and peace times.

International Small Craft Center *(opposite)*

Opened in 2003, the International Small Craft Center is a new addition to the Mariners' Museum. It features a collection of 150 small boats from 36 countries. An elevated path leads through eleven areas with themes such as *culture* and *shape*.

Ship Modeling (*above*)

A professional model builder creates a ship for the museum's extraordinary collection of historically accurate reproductions, featuring every type of vessel ever constructed. They range in size from a tiny Chinese sampan model to a 33-foot-long replica of the Queen Elizabeth.

Mariners' Museum Playground (*left*)

A small child sits in the portal of a wooden play ship outside of the Mariners' Museum. The museum's woodland park setting features a five-mile hiking trail around Lake Maury.

Exquisite Craftsmanship (*opposite*)

Seafaring enthusiasts can spend hours touring the fascinating collections of over 2000 handcrafted ship models, paintings, rare figureheads, and authentic items from the Civil War ironclad, *U.S.S. Monitor*. The Mariners' Museum has over 60,000 square feet of gallery space.

Village Theatre (above)

Originally a movie theater, the Village Theatre in Newport News now houses the Peninsula Community Theatre for the Performing Arts. The original Art Deco marquee and building design are a lasting tribute to an era gone by.

Virginia War Museum (opposite)

Since 1923 the Virginia War Museum in Newport News has collected over 60,000 artifacts of which only five percent can be viewed at one time due to limited space. The prolific collection covers America's military history from 1775 to the present.

Lee Hall Mansion, Newport News

Wealthy planter Richard D. Lee built this Italianate mansion in 1859. Three years later, the Lee family fled their new home as Union troops advanced upon them in the first battles of the Civil War. Today the fully-restored mansion is the only large, antebellum plantation house left on the lower Virginia Peninsula. Guided tours give a detailed perspective of plantation life and the Union Army's 1862 Peninsula Campaign.

Ferguson Center for the Arts *(top)*

The Ferguson Center is the pride of Christopher Newport University. Designed by architect, I.M. Pei, it hosts some of the world's finest performers in a 1700-seat proscenium theatre, as well as more intimate 450-seat and 125-seat theatres.

Christopher Newport University *(bottom)*

This nationally acclaimed institution was founded in 1960 in Newport News as a two-year branch of the venerable College of William and Mary (chartered 1693). Even though it is the youngest comprehensive university in Virginia, it has been on a fast-track of excellence. In 1999, *U.S. News & World Report* ranked the school number two among regional public liberal arts colleges in the South in its *America's Best Colleges*.

Rose Garden at Huntington Park

Located on a bluff overlooking the James River, this scenic park in Newport News showcases a landscaped rose garden with forty-five different bloom varieties. The grounds also feature Fort Fun, a 15,000-square-foot wooden playground.

Warwick Boulevard Shops

The quaint residential architecture of Newport News' Huntington Heights community
is also home to a variety of charming shops.
Listed on the National Register of Historic
Places, this neighborhood has many lovely
homes built in the 1920's.

Schooner Alliance, Yorktown

Experience sailing's golden age aboard this
105-foot, three-masted schooner that
departs from Yorktown's Riverwalk Landing.
As the vessel's billowy sails fill with salty
breezes, voyagers can view dolphins,
seabirds, and historic sites along the coast.

Watermen's Museum *(left and right)*

Situated on the shores of the York River, Watermen's Museum was founded in 1981 during the 200th anniversary celebration of the Battle of Yorktown, the final battle of the Revolutionary War. The museum honors the heritage of the Chesapeake Bay's *watermen*, an ancient title for those who make their living at sea. The term is still used today in England as well as in the Chesapeake area. The museum features the history of local fishing from Native American times to the present.

Victory Monument (*opposite*)

Overlooking the York River, the female figure of Victory stands proudly atop this ninety-eight-foot-tall monument, a tribute to the brave soldiers who fought and won the last great battle of the American Revolution.

Historic Yorktown Battlefield (*above*)

The Yorktown Battlefield is the famed site of the battle that ended the American Revolutionary War and secured America's freedom from England in 1781. History buffs can tour the battle's siege lines, complete with cannons, the field where British General Cornwallis surrendered, the Nelson House, a museum of artifacts including George Washington's field tent, and the town of York.

Yorktown Victory Center *(top and bottom)*

The Yorktown Victory Center chronicles America's history from colonial times to independence, with an emphasis on Yorktown's role as a decisive battleground of the Revolutionary War. A 1780's farm depicts early-American life during the decade after independence was won, while a re-created Continental Army camp characterizes the daily life of soldiers at the end of the American Revolution.

Historic Yorktown *(opposite)*

Historic Yorktown, with the Coleman Memorial Bridge beyond, is part of the *Historic Triangle* that includes Yorktown, Jamestown, and Williamsburg. All three are 17th-century colonial villages where living history is enacted every day for tourists.

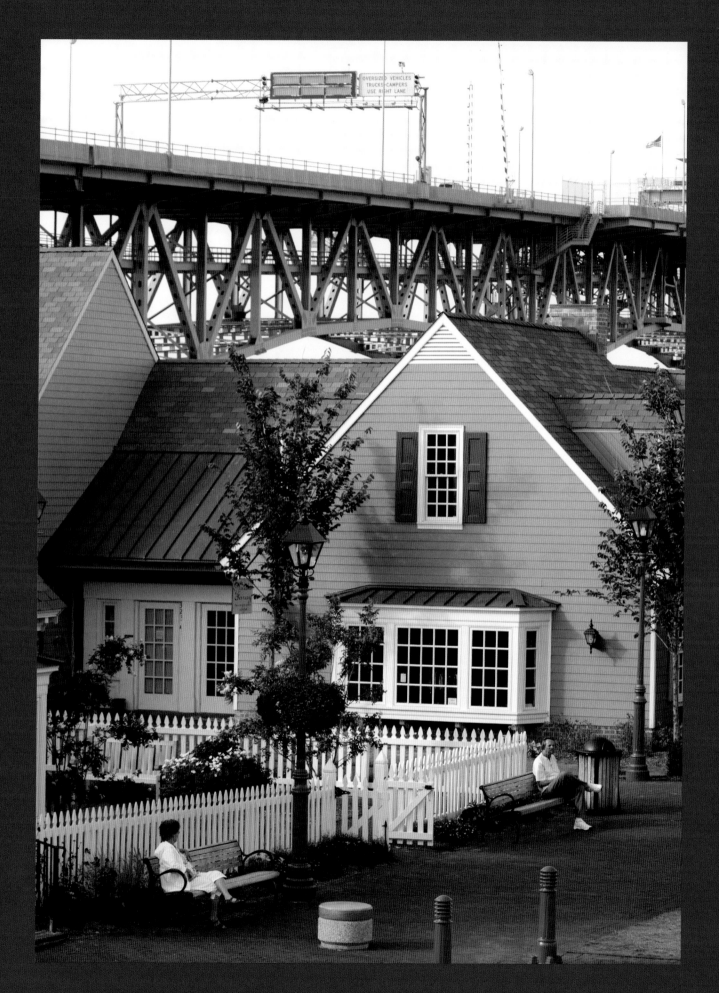

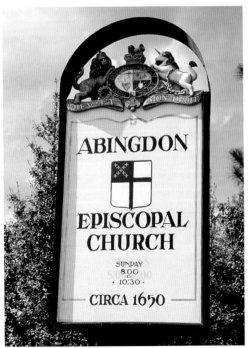

Abingdon Episcopal Church *(above and left)*

The largest of eight colonial churches in Virginia, Abingdon Episcopal Church was established in 1650 in Gloucester. The current church, on the same site, was built in 1755 in a rare, Latin crucifix design. The earliest graves in the church cemetery date back to the mid-1650's and include the final resting places of Revolutionary and Confederate War soldiers. These raised monuments mark family graves that were moved to the church cemetery in 1911.

Historic Gloucester

A tobacco-producing area in colonial times, Gloucester is also known as the site of General Cornwallis' "Second Surrender," after his defeat at nearby Yorktown. Gloucester's old plantation homes and private estates are open to the public, especially during Historic Garden Week in April. Beginning with English daffodil bulbs brought over by colonists, the spring flower became a flourishing industry, making Gloucester County the *Daffodil Capital of America* by the 20th century.

Jamestown Settlement (top)

In 1607, thirteen years before the Pilgrims landed at Plymouth Rock, 101 men and 4 boys, the only survivors of a difficult Atlantic crossing, established a settlement that became America's earliest permanent English colony.

James River Ferry (bottom)

In 1925, the Jamestown-Scotland Ferry was the first automobile ferryboat to cross the James River. The scenic ride connects Jamestown with Scotland, Virginia. It is the only 24-hour ferry operation in Virginia that is state-run.

Captain John Smith (opposite)

President of the Jamestown Colony in 1607, Captain John Smith played an integral leadership role in the formation of Jamestown. Illness sent him back to England in 1609, but he returned to America in 1614 to map the New England coast.

Colonial Jamestown (*top*)

The Visitors Center encompasses the world of early Jamestown with exhibits of 17th-century artifacts and a documentary film that explores the settlement's beginnings and interactions with their Algonquin neighbors.

Powhatan Indian Village (*bottom and opposite*)

The powerful Chief Powhatan was father to Princess Pocahontas, who intervened to save Captain John Smith from execution by the Powhatan tribe leader. A recreation of the Algonquin chief's village has mound-shaped, reed-covered houses, a ceremonial dance circle, a garden, and a cooking pit. Animal skins had many important uses for Virginia's Native Americans. Here skins are dried and stretched on a rack to be made into clothing, water pouches or bedding.

Colonial Greeting (top)

A James Fort guard greets a settler at the front gate, just one of many interactions among costumed historical interpreters that portray the rhythm of daily life in America's first continuous English settlement.

Colonial Military Gear (bottom)

James Fort visitors are invited to participate in colonial activities such as forging metal objects, sewing, and preparing a meal. They can also try on helmets and armor and watch costumed performers fire their muskets.

Inside the Palisades

Thatched-roof houses inside the triangular wooden palisades of James Fort are authentically constructed with the wattle-and-daub technique. The builder sets the walls with wooden stakes (wattles) and daubs or covers them with a mixture of clay and sand. Other dwellings at the fort include a church, guardhouse, storehouse, and governor's house, all authentically reproduced to reflect the early years of Jamestown, 1610–1614.

Susan Constant (above)

The *Susan Constant* is a replica of one of the three ships that brought America's earliest European ancestors from England to Virginia under the sparsest of conditions in 1607. The ship can be boarded at Jamestown Settlement's pier.

Discovery (opposite)

The *Discovery* was the smallest of three ships that brought the first adventurous men and boys to Jamestown. Remarkably, these modest sailing ships made it across thousands of miles of rough Atlantic waters. In preparation for Jamestown's four-hundredth anniversary celebration in 2007, the third ship, *Godspeed*, sailed to six ports between Old Town Alexandria, Virginia and Newport, Rhode Island in May, 2006.

Photos above and opposite reprinted with permission from The Colonial Williamsburg Foundation

Colonial Williamsburg *(above)*

It is the eve of the American Revolution and the tension is high in the town of Williamsburg, the new colonial capital of Virginia, where a young country is defining its courage and beliefs. History comes alive with historical reenactments and depictions of authentic figures such as (*left to right*) Gowan Pamphlet, a slave and founder of a black church; Thomas Jefferson; Lydia Broadnax, a slave cook for George Wythe; and Patrick Henry.

History Comes to Life *(opposite)*

Colonial Williamsburg is a first-rate adventure back in time. A cast of historical interpreters relive Colonial America on the brink of revolution surrounded by more than 500 restored and reconstructed buildings on hundreds of acres of land.

The College of William & Mary (*top*)

The second oldest college in America, this stately university in Williamsburg was granted a charter by King William III and Queen Mary II in 1693. Since its inception, the Ivy League college has continued to be highly acclaimed.

Christopher Wren Building (*bottom*)

The oldest academic building still in use (1693), was designed by famed architect Christopher Wren and was the first building on the William & Mary campus. It also housed political activities during Jamestown's days as the state capitol.

Norborne Berkeley Statue

Norborne Berkeley, an English baron, was governor of Virginia from 1768 to 1770 and served on the board of the College of William & Mary. He resided in the Governor's Palace, a major attraction at Colonial Williamsburg.

The Williamsburg Winery (above)

Tours and tasting events are offered at the Williamsburg Winery, the largest winery in Virginia. During the tour, the fascinating winemaking process is revealed and the different vintages from this award-winning winery can be sampled.

First Landing State Park (opposite)

Spanish moss cascades from tree limbs at First Landing State Park, the most northern location in the country where this moss can be found. The park's hiking trails meander through a unique habitat of lagoons, cypress trees, and rare plants. The first settlers of Jamestown landed at this site on April 26, 1607, then continued up the James River to establish the permanent settlement of Jamestown.

Floating Museum

Off Granby Street in Norfolk, the *U.S.S. Wisconsin* creates an interesting landscape illusion. Actually afloat at nearby docks, she is one of the most decorated battle ships in the history of warfare, earning six battle stars, five in World War II alone.

U.S.S. Wisconsin

On December 17th, 1944, just a year after being launched, the *U.S.S. Wisconsin* miraculously survived a typhoon in the Pacific Ocean. The *Wisconsin* was the largest and last great battle ship commissioned by the U.S. Navy.

National Maritime Museum (*top and bottom*)

The National Maritime Museum is a stirring attraction on the Norfolk waterfront that explores the military, economic, and environmental impact of the sea on the Norfolk community. It includes Nauticus, a marine-themed science center, the *U.S.S.* *Wisconsin* floating museum, the Hampton Roads Naval Museum, the NOAA@Nauticus, education resource center, and the Cruise Norfolk terminal, Virginia's homeport for the booming Caribbean cruise business.

The Homecoming (*opposite*)

An emotional homecoming of a chief petty officer is depicted in this bronze in Town Point Park. This statue and *The Lone Sailor*, in Wisconsin square, were donated by the U.S. Navy Memorial Foundation. Both have sister statues in Washington, D.C.

U.S.S. *Wisconsin*

First deployed in 1944, the *U.S.S. Wisconsin* still features six of her original nine 16-inch guns that fire shells weighing over one ton apiece. Three were removed to add Tomahawk and Harpoon missiles before deployment to the Persian Gulf in 1990.

Military Might

The *U.S.S.* *Wisconsin*'s main gun battery
has a range of 23 miles while her second
gun battery has a range of over 9 miles.
She is one of three U.S. Navy battleships
that remain candidates for reactivation.

Chesapeake Bay Bridge-Tunnel (above)

Connecting Virginia's eastern shore to the Virginia mainland at Virginia Beach, this 20-mile-long bridge-tunnel complex is considered one of the seven engineering wonders of the modern world.

Chesapeake Bay Fishing (opposite, top)

The vast wetlands and waterways of the Chesapeake Bay are filled with an unmatched variety of marine life for commercial fishermen, serious anglers, and even novice seamen.

American Rover Tour (opposite, bottom)

Inspired by the design of elegant, 19th-century schooners, the *American Rover* relives the thrill of sailing the Elizabeth River as it felt over one hundred years ago. The schooner sets sail on morning, noon, and sunset tours.

Naval Station Norfolk

The world's largest naval base sits on 4,300 acres of the Sewell's Point peninsula in Hampton Roads. It is home to 134 aircraft and 75 ships, including aircraft carriers, cruisers, destroyers, amphibious ships, and the Department of the Navy's supply and logistics ships, aircraft, and helicopters. The base supports U.S. Naval Operations in the Atlantic Ocean, Mediterranean Sea and Indian Ocean.

Catching Norfolk's Character

Dwarfed by the imposing aircraft carrier *U.S.S. Theodore Roosevelt* beyond the jetty, sport fishermen enjoy an afternoon on the waters of Hampton Roads. The ever-present ships are a large part of the personality of this unique setting.

Old Dominion Sailboat Team *(above)*

The Old Dominion University sailing team practices maneuvers and hones their seamanship skills on the challenging waters of the busy Elizabeth River. National champions, this team of winners is getting used to crossing the finish line first.

Dress Whites *(opposite)*

Sailors in service dress whites line the decks of the *U.S.S. Porter* (DDG 78) arriving at her berth in Norfolk, guided by the tug, *Marci Moran*. Commissioned in 1999, the guided missile destroyer is the fifth U.S. Naval ship to bear the name *U.S.S Porter.*

The Elizabeth River (*top and bottom*)

As smaller boats enjoy a leisurely day on the river, it's all business on the working docks of the Elizabeth River. Above, a fully-loaded container ship fires up its engine and prepares to leave. Below, a giant crane is in the process of lowering containers onto the deck of a commercial ship. The Norfolk International Terminals is the largest terminal of the Virginia Port Authority.

Loading Coal (*opposite*)

Handling sixty-five million tons per year, these coal-loading docks are the most modern and efficient in the world. Each year, 2,700 ships load at these facilities, making Hampton Roads the ninth busiest port in the country.

Barge on the Lafayette

Marine traffic on the Lafayette River is always varied and interesting, as commercial ships and barges pass private recreational boats, sightseeing boats, and military ships.

Norfolk Yacht & Country Club

This historic country club on the Lafayette River opened in 1896, creating a gracious and elegant setting for its members. NYCC hosts annual regattas and has a health club, swimming pools, tennis courts, and restaurants.

Life on the Lafayette River (*above*)

The flowing rivers that feed into Hampton
Roads and the great Chesapeake Bay create
some of the most beautiful riverfront real
estate in Virginia. This quiet cove on the
Lafayette River shows the tranquil intimacy
of waterside living.

Shores of Isle of Wight County (*opposite*)

Established in 1634, the beautiful Isle of
Wight County, along the western banks of
the James River, is one of the original eight
shires, or counties, in Virginia. The lush,
manicured lawns of many historic homes
and mansions reach down to the river's
edge making it one of the most coveted and
venerable neighborhoods in the Tidewater
area. The rhythmic pattern along the shoreline is created by stone jetties that prevent
beach erosion and protect the shoreline
from wind and the wakes of passing boats.

Sunset on Willoughby Spit *(opposite)*

A magnificent sunset paints the sky over Willoughby Spit, a peninsula of land marking the southern entrance to Chesapeake Bay that is bordered by Willoughby Bay to the south and Hampton Roads to the west.

Fishing at Oceanview Pier *(top and bottom)*

The view is spectacular and the fishing is great from Norfolk's new Oceanview Pier on Willoughby Spit. The waters are flush with croaker, spot, bluefish, flounder, trout, and striper, to name a few. Historically, the seven-mile-long Willoughby Spit appeared overnight, created by the primal forces of the Great Coastal Hurricane of 1806. Since that time, breakwaters were created to protect it from likely destruction by future hurricane forces along Atlantic shores.

Hermitage Foundation Museum

Situated on impeccably landscaped
grounds, complete with rose gardens and
statuary, the Hermitage Museum presents
the lifestyle and art collection of the
wealthy Sloane family during the first
half of the 20th century.

Hermitage Gardens

The historic Hermitage Museum is tucked away in a residential neighborhood in Norfolk. Originally built in 1895 as a five-room vacation home for wealthy New Yorkers, William and Florence Sloane, it was expanded over time to forty-two rooms after the family moved to Norfolk permanently. Serious fine art collectors, the Sloanes founded the city's Society of Arts and first art museum, which became the Chrysler Museum of Art.

Federal-style Architecture *(opposite)*

The precise details of this Norfolk town-house entranceway in the Freemason district beautifully illustrate the popular Federal-style architecture that flowered during the early decades of a newly independent America.

Norfolk Botanical Gardens *(above)*

Deep-purple tulips adorn the Sarah Lee Baker Perennial Garden. The centerpiece of the one-acre garden is a limestone fountain and terraced canals that create the tranquil sound of gently flowing water, surrounded by over two-hundred varieties of perennials, annuals and ornamental shrubs. The Baker Family funded many features throughout the Norfolk Botanical Gardens with their generous donations.

Rotunda at the Gardens

Edged with blooming rhododendrons, the
Norfolk Botanical Gardens Rotunda is one
of several indoor facilities for private or
corporate events. Overlooking a patio and
fountain in the heart of the gardens, it is
a rainy-day site for outdoor weddings.

Nature's Brushstrokes (top)

In this idyllic scene, an artist captures the beauty of these lush gardens with her paintbrush. Nature's palette of brilliant shapes and colors has always beckoned painters to re-create the area's exceptional landscapes on canvas.

Rhododendrons in Bloom (bottom)

The original blooms that were planted in 1938 consisted of 2,000 rhododendrons, 4,000 azaleas, several thousand shrubs and trees, and 100 bushels of daffodils. Since then, the gardens have grown in size and beauty.

Flowing Lion (*above*)

The numerous gardens of the Norfolk Botanical Gardens are accented with small and large fountains, reflecting pools, playful fountain decorations and famous historic statues showcased in The Statuary Vista area.

An American Artist in Europe (*opposite*)

The Statuary Vista is an elegantly beautiful outdoor sculpture garden. It features a promenade lined by 19th-century marble figures of well-known European artists and one American artist, Thomas Crawford, famous for his impressive *Statue of Freedom* at the U.S. Capitol dome. The pieces depict artists such as Rembrandt, Rubens, Canova, Phidias, Murillo, Durer and DaVinci; all statues were sculpted by Sir Moses Jacob Ezekiel.

The World Trade Center (*top*)

Norfolk's World Trade Center hosts a variety of international service providers under one roof, including customs brokers, freight forwarders, international companies and government agencies. It is one of 241 such centers in sixty countries.

Norfolk Waterfront (*bottom*)

Norfolk's historic downtown waterfront, on the scenic Elizabeth River, features waterfront restaurants, shops, the Chrysler Art Museum, and the Nauticus Maritime Museum as well as ferries and sightseeing boats.

The Confederate Monument (*opposite*)

This 1907 statue in Norfolk's financial district commemorates the last reunion of Confederate Civil War survivors. The likeness of a young Confederate soldier stands fifteen feet in the air atop a white granite pedestal.

The MacArthur Memorial *(above)*

The memorial to World War II's renowned General Douglas MacArthur consists of four buildings in MacArthur Square: archives, library, research center, and a rotunda where he and his wife are buried.

Owen B. Pickett U.S. Customhouse *(opposite, top)*

Norfolk was one of the first ports in the nation to have an official U.S. Customs Office. Other than a short time during the Civil War, it has served Norfolk since 1858.

Tribute to a Hero *(opposite, bottom)*

The hub of the MacArthur Memorial Complex is the restored 1850 Norfolk City Hall which is home to the Jean MacArthur (Mrs. Douglas MacArthur) Research Center, housing the general's archived memorabilia.

Harrison Opera House

Home of the Virginia Opera Company, the
Harrison Opera House was once a World
War II USO theater. Newly renovated with
elaborate chandeliers and grand, sweeping
staircases, its elegant charm evokes a
gracious bygone era.

The Chrysler Museum of Art *(top)*

Founded in 1939, the museum's collection grew dramatically when automobile heir and art collector Walter P. Chrysler, Jr. donated his collection to the city of Norfolk. Today more than 30,000 objects span nearly 4,000 years of art history.

The Wells Theatre *(bottom)*

This 1912 beaux-arts opera house was originally a burlesque and vaudeville theater owned by the famous Wells brothers. It is now home to the Virginia Stage Company, a nationally recognized professional theater group.

Old Dominion University (top)

Old Dominion University was honored in 2005 as one of the best colleges in the Southeast by The Princeton Review. A handsomely landscaped campus, with tree-lined walkways, creates a small-college feel for this respected institution.

Friendship Park (bottom)

Friendship Park was a gift to Norfolk from the government of China in 1983. Also known as *Pagoda Park*, this idyllic down-town oasis is beautifully cultivated with profuse gardens and an authentic Koi pond.

Waterside Festival Marketplace (opposite)

Located along the banks of the Elizabeth River in downtown Norfolk, Waterside is a real festival of shopping, dining, and enter-tainment. After the sun goes down, the night life starts up at five different clubs.

Epworth Methodist Church *(above)*

Services in the original church building of the Norfolk Epworth Methodist congregation began in 1848. By 1894, the present building was completed in the dramatic Romanesque architectural style. The bell tower chimes play daily at noon.

Freemason Street Baptist Church *(opposite)*

Thomas U. Walter, renowned 19th-century architect of the U.S. Capitol dome, designed the stunning Gothic-Revival sanctuary of this historic Baptist church, built in 1848, in downtown Norfolk.

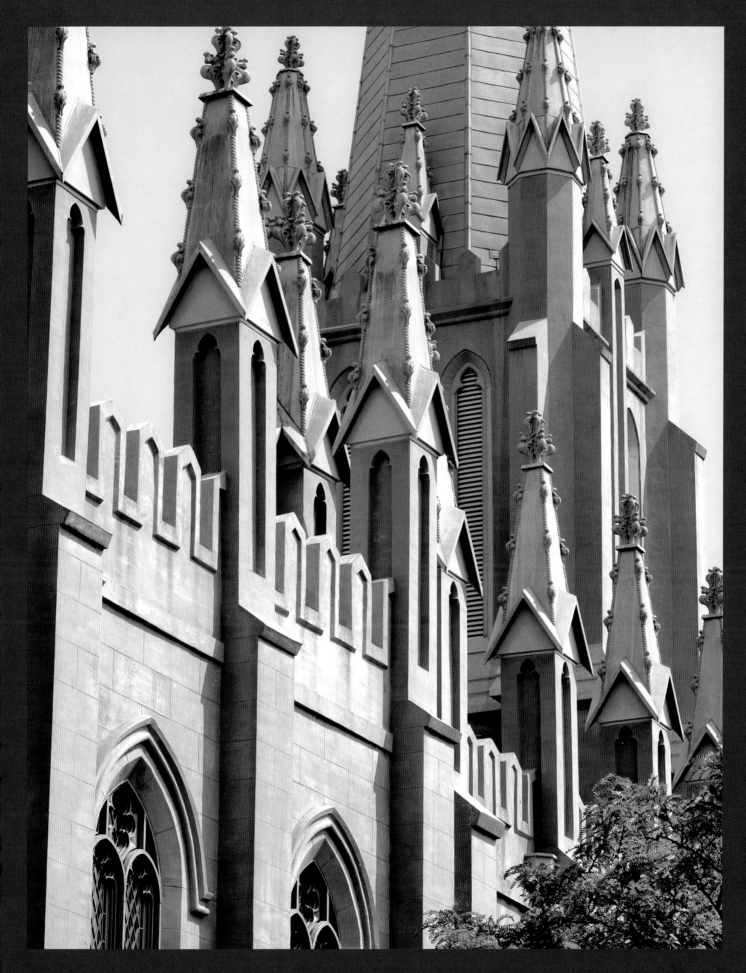

Norfolk Academy (above)

Norfolk Academy was founded in 1728, making it the oldest secondary school in Virginia and the eighth oldest in the United States. A college preparatory school for boys, it merged with the Country Day School for Girls in 1966.

Loyal Mascot (opposite)

A statue of Norfolk Academy's beloved bulldog mascot is poised on the rim of the fountain. The highly-acclaimed private academy serves grades one through twelve and is recognized for academic excellence.

Chrysler Hall Performing Arts Center (*top*)

Part of the Scope complex, the elegant, 2300-seat Chrysler Hall is Norfolk's top performance hall and home to the Virginia Symphony. The center hosts popular Broadway shows and world class artists.

Norfolk Scope Arena (*bottom*)

Home to the Norfolk Admirals professional hockey team and Arena Racing USA, the Scope Arena hosts a variety of events, including national rock concert tours and popular family shows like the Ringling Brothers and Barnum and Bailey Circus.

The Virginia Zoological Park

The Virginia Zoological Park's nearly four hundred inhabitants consist of Siberian tigers, elephants, monkeys, reptiles, and birds. The new Africa exhibit added nine new species, including zebras, lions, meerkats, and these exquisite giraffes.

Moses Meyer House and Garden (*opposite*)

This Federal-style house and its gardens in Norfolk are administered by the Chrysler Museum of Art as a showplace of what life was like at the turn of the 18th century. Family portraits by acclaimed artist, Gilbert Stuart grace the walls.

Historic Willoughby-Baylor House (*above*)

The Norfolk History Museum at the Willoughby-Baylor House offers tours of the refurbished Federal-style townhouse that incorporates local decorative arts of the period and presentations on historical buildings and events throughout Norfolk. Built in 1794, the home was originally owned by Captain William Willoughby and later by the Baylor family.

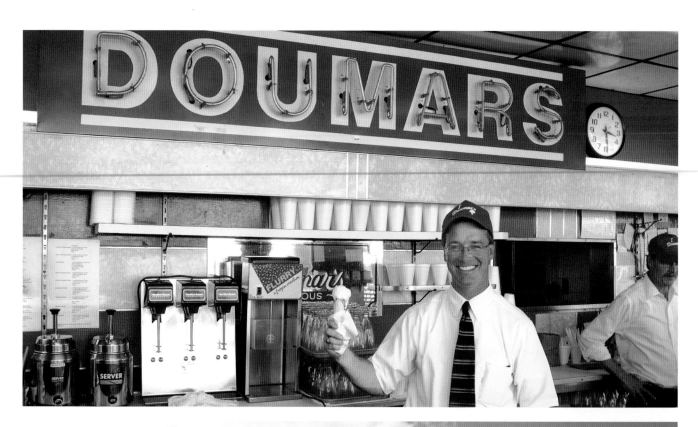

Doumar's Cones and Barbecue

(top and bottom)

Doumar's Cones and Barbecue is a staple
in Norfolk. Opened in 1934, it's the longest
running drive-in restaurant in America and
the home of the first ice cream cone
machine.

Vintage Ads on Granby Street

Ads that were freshly painted on a downtown building in the 1950's, reflect Virginia Beach's ongoing connection with its three military bases: Oceana Naval Air Station, the Naval Amphibious Base Little Creek, and Fort Story Army Base.

The Virginia Aquarium and Marine Science Center (top and opposite)

The mosaic dolphin sculpture in front of the aquarium is a tribute to *A Dolphin's Promise*, a non-profit organization that raises money for the Lance Armstrong Livestrong Foundation for cancer research. Ten-percent of the proceeds benefit the Aquarium's efforts to rescue and study stranded sea animals. Throughout the year, the center offers boating excursions to watch dolphins and whales, and to study marine life.

Virginia Aquarium (left)

A curious sea turtle investigates delighted onlookers at the Virginia Aquarium. One of the nation's top-ten aquariums, this acclaimed Virginia Beach attraction show-cases the complex variety of marine life in the mid-Atlantic and Chesapeake Bay.

Bell House (above)

The Bell House is a lovely example of the region's 19th-century residential architecture. Built circa 1820, the home currently serves as the official residence of the commanding officer of the Oceana Naval Air Station.

Flame of Hope (opposite)

The eternal flame is an ever-present visual commemorative of Vietnam's POW's and MIA's. The memorial is located near the entrance to Oceana Naval Air Station in Virginia Beach, where jets can be seen during their take off.

FLAME OF HOPE
THIS FLAME WILL BURN CONTINUOUSLY
TO LIGHT THE WAY FOR THE RETURN
OF OUR PRISONERS OF WAR HELD IN
SOUTH EAST ASIA

DEDICATED BY
CONCERNED CITIZENS AND
SERVICEMEN OF THE
AREA

Cavalier Hotels of Virginia Beach *(top)*

The historic Cavalier-on-the-Hill opened in 1927 and attracted wealthy vacationers who arrived at the hotel's own train stop. Now, with its modern counterpart, Cavalier-on-the-Ocean, the tradition of excellence continues.

The Edgar Cayce Institute *(bottom)*

Founded in 1931 by controversial psychic and healer Edgar Cayce, The Association for Research and Enlightenment began in this building. The educational organization outgrew this original space and is now located in new quarters.

**World Headquarters for
Psychic Research**

In the late 19th century, a Kentuckian named Edgar Cayce realized he could enter a meditative state and answer questions people posed on any given subject. Over the next forty-five years, Cayce performed thousands of documented readings. His psychic work has been carried on at the Institute's international headquarters in Virginia Beach.

The Neptune Festival (*top and bottom*)

A row of exquisitely detailed sandcastles line the beach as far as the eye can see during the festival's much-anticipated sand-sculpting competition. The region's finest artisans create their masterpieces safely out of the tide's reach.

The Ultimate Sandcastle (*opposite*)

The Neptune Festival, which began in 1973, has blossomed into one of the top ten festivals on the east coast. It begins in March with a gala, and events continue from May through September, including the popular sand-sculpting competition.

Mount Trashmore Park (top and bottom)

The City of Virginia Beach transformed solid waste disposal into a beautiful recreational park with creativity, style and a sense of humor. Aptly named *Mount Trashmore,* the 62-foot-high mountain features the *City Seal of Virginia Beach,* bike trails, a skate park, walking and jogging paths, picnic areas, and two freshwater lakes stocked with fish. It is a recycling wonder.

A Shoreline Playground (opposite)

Virginia Beach draws its share of enthusiastic surfers and boogie boarders. Beyond the waves, a catamaran searches for a breeze, as sailors and beach-goers soak in the sunshine.

Naval Aviation Monument, Monument Park *(above and left)*

Virginia Beach is home to Naval Air Station Oceana, the largest master jet fighter base for Tomcats and Hornets in the United States. This monument, by Oregon sculptor Michael Maiden, pays tribute to the U.S. Navy's airmen and the area's rich aviation heritage.

Norwegian Lady *(opposite)*

The *Norwegian Lady* in Monument Park is a gift from the people of Norway commemorating the 1891 shipwreck of the Norwegian barque, *Dictator*, and the rescue of eight crewmen by the local Coast Guard. The turbulent Virginia-North Carolina coast is known as the "Graveyard of the Atlantic" for the 2,000 sunken ships in the region.

I AM
THE NORWEGIAN LADY

I STAND HERE
AS MY SISTER BEFORE ME
TO WISH ALL MEN OF THE SEA
SAFE RETURN HOME

The Sailors' Lifeline *(above and left)*

This historic 1915 Coast Guard station on the Virginia Beach boardwalk is now a museum that showcases lifesaving equipment of the early 20th century, exhibits artifacts from the Norwegian ship, *Dictator*, and offers educational programs.

Atlantic Wildfowl Heritage Museum
(above)

The Atlantic Wildfowl Heritage Museum is located in the DeWitt Cottage, the oldest oceanfront cottage in Virginia Beach. The center shares information on migratory wildfowl that pass through the mid-Atlantic coast with woodcarvings, art and artifacts.

New Cape Henry Lighthouse *(right)*

In the Tidewater area of Virginia, where American history goes back four hundred years, it's not surprising that the "new" Cape Henry Lighthouse is over 100 years old and the old lighthouse, in the background, dates back to 1792.

Beacon of Light *(opposite)*

Old Glory flies in a brisk Atlantic wind on the keeper's cottage of the new Cape Henry Lighthouse. The cast-iron tower features a light that can be seen nineteen miles from shore.

A Tale of Two Lighthouses *(above)*

Adjacent to its replacement, the old Cape Henry Light was the first lighthouse built by a young American government to make the Chesapeake Bay safe and navigable.

King Neptune, God of the Sea

This massive bronze statue of Neptune was funded by Virginia Beach's highly acclaimed Neptune Festival and created by noted Richmond sculptor Paul DiPasquale. The finished work of art stands a royal twenty-six feet tall. Trident in hand, the muscular Neptune is surrounded by the creatures of his realm, a seventeen-foot dolphin, an eleven-foot loggerhead turtle, an eight-foot octopus, and other creatures of the deep.

Virginia Beach Fishing Pier

Scenic Virginia Beach Fishing Pier at 15th Street and Atlantic Avenue, juts out one-thousand feet over the ocean. With exceptional deep-sea fishing venues, Virginia Beach is ranked one of the top 25 fishing destinations by *Field and Stream* magazine.

Life's a Beach-Ball

A popular oceanside resort, beautiful
Virginia Beach has a personality all its own.
The historic boardwalk is scattered with
giant sculptures of beach balls, sand cas-
tles, sea turtles, and the Roman god
Neptune.

Virginia Beach *(top and bottom)*

Virginia Beach is a fabulous summer vacation spot where frolicking in the waves and soaking up the sun's rays is highly encouraged. In addition, visitors may appreciate the city's wide variety of restaurants and shops along its three-mile boardwalk.

125

Charter Boats (above)

A great day in Virginia Beach begins aboard a charter boat on Lake Rudee, then heading out the Rudee Inlet for a memorable day of deep-sea fishing in search of native wahoo or yellow-fin tuna and other species that migrate along the coast.

Rudee Inlet (bottom)

At day's end, when deep-sea fishing boats return to their slips on Lake Rudee, the docks are abuzz with excitement as anglers weigh in their catches and lament about the big ones that got away.

Oceanfront Paradise (opposite)

Hotels, condos, and cottages line the prime oceanfront property of Virginia Beach, providing a variety of wonderful seaside resort accomodations. Rudee Inlet cuts across the beach, providing easy access from Lake Rudee.

Jake McGuire is known for his striking photos of American cities and landscapes. His photos appear in private collections, exhibitions, offices, and are often found in airline and travel magazines. He has won 11 awards for photography and photojournalism. In January of 1989, the Presidential Inaugural Committee commissioned McGuire to produce a signed, limited edition print of the White House. It was signed by the President and Vice President and given to those who performed at the Inaugural Gala. In March of 1992, McGuire received an Arts America grant from the United States Information Agency to give photography lectures in the Persian Gulf Sheikdom of Bahrain. In April of 1997, *LIFE MAGAZINE* selected one of McGuire's photos for the cover of a special edition of *LIFE*. In August of 2004, McGuire joined forces with Twin Lights Publishers to produce a series of colorful photographic journals. Titles that are currently available include, *Washington, D.C.: A Photographic Portrait, Baltimore, MD: A Photographic Portrait,* and *Annapolis, MD: A Photographic Portrait.* He is also working on a book on the coast of New England to be released in the spring of 2007 by Twin Lights Publishers. See more of Jake's work at www.TheMcGuireCollection.com.